MATHS

TEN STEPS to improve your child's ADDING AND SUBTRACTING for ages 8-9

Step 1	Adding tens	2
Step 2	Adding hundreds	4
Step 3	Adding 9 and 99	6
Step 4	Adding tens and ones	8
Step 5	Subtracting tens and ones	12
Step 6	Adding hundreds, tens and ones	16
Step 7	Subtracting hundreds, tens and ones	20
Step 8	Solving problems using addition and subtraction	24
Step 9	Working with fractions	26
Step 10	Adding decimals	28

Parents' pages 30

AUTHOR Ian Gardner
ILLUSTRATOR Garry Davies

Let's learn at home

Step 1: Adding tens

This step will help you to work with multiples of 10.

1 ten = 10	10
2 tens = 10 + 10	20
3 tens =	
4 tens =	
5 tens =	
6 tens =	
7 tens =	
8 tens =	
9 tens =	
10 tens =	

'Multiples' are numbers which divide into equal sets. 3 sets of 10 are 30, so 30 is a multiple of 10.

◀ Carry on this pattern by writing a multiple of 10 on each step of the staircase.

Arrange the numbers 20, 30, 40, 50 and 60 each time so that the horizontal and vertical totals match the target total below. The centre numbers have already been placed for you.

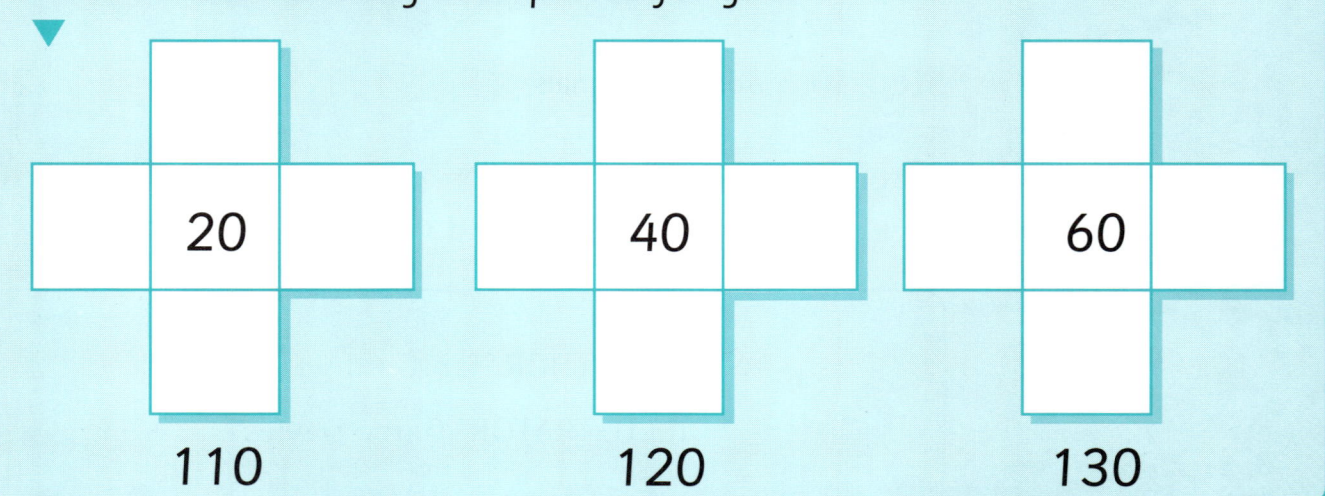

▼

20		40		60
110		120		130

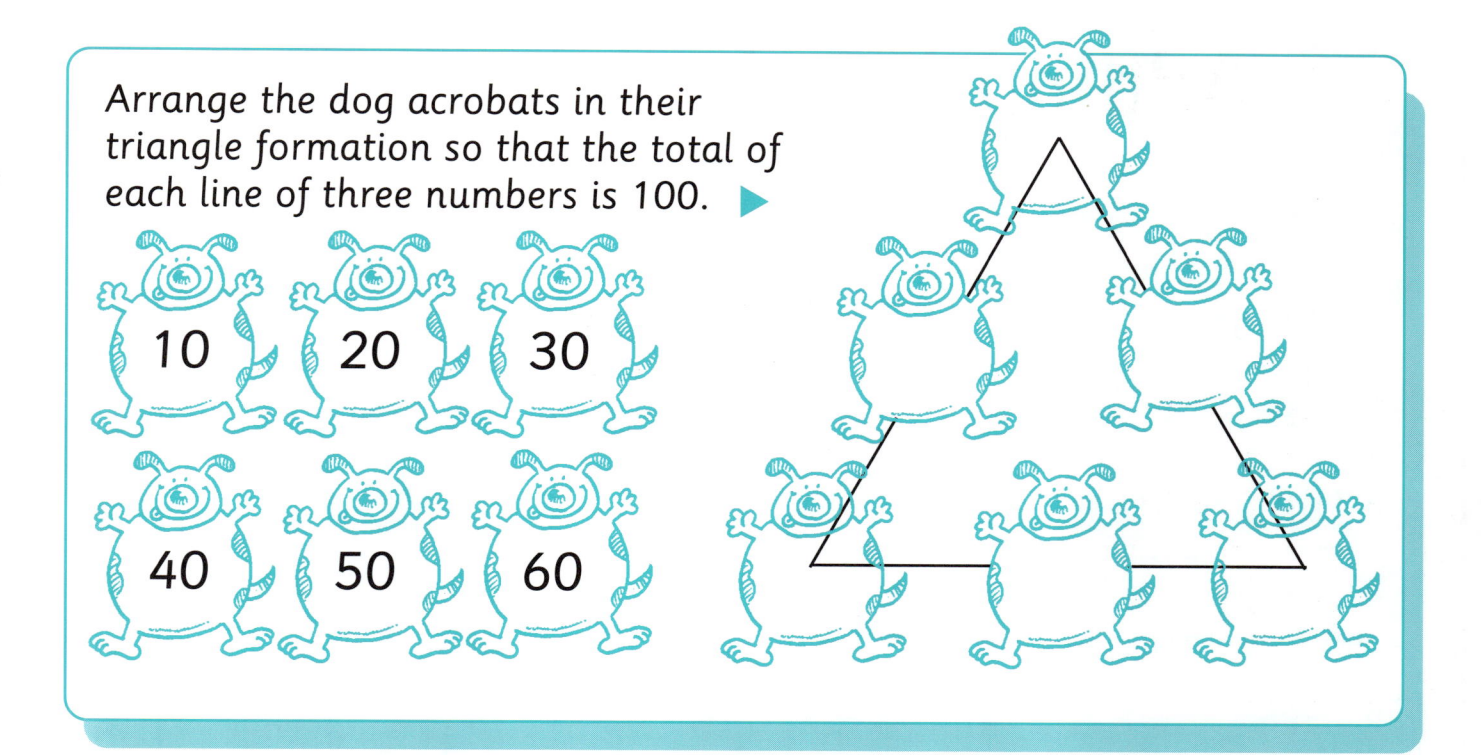

Arrange the dog acrobats in their triangle formation so that the total of each line of three numbers is 100. ▶

10 20 30
40 50 60

Continue these sums.
▼

10 + 10 = 20
20 + 20 = ☐
30 + ☐ = 60
☐ + ☐ = ☐
☐ + ☐ = ☐
☐ + ☐ = ☐
☐ + ☐ = ☐
☐ + ☐ = ☐
☐ + ☐ = ☐

Is there a pattern in the answers? Tell an adult.

Adding tens together isn't that much harder than adding ones. If you managed the triangle puzzle above, see if you can rearrange the dogs to make these totals:
- each line making 90;
- each line making 110;
- each line making 120.

When you finish this step put a sticker here!

Dear Parent or Carer

This step contains some basic activities that involve building numbers or solving problems. Being able to add tens easily will be particularly useful for your child when he or she is working out everyday problems mentally. For example, to add 63p and 63p in your head, a simple way is to work out that 60 + 60 = 120 and 3 + 3 = 6, so 63p + 63p = 126p or £1.26. The answers are given on page 30.

Step 2: Adding hundreds

This step will help you to add hundreds, going up to and beyond 1000.

Ten ones = 1 + 1 + 1 + 1 + 1 + 1 + 1 + 1 + 1 + 1 = 10

Ten tens = ☐ + ☐ + ☐ + ☐ + ☐ + ☐ + ☐ + ☐ + ☐ + ☐ = ☐

Ten hundreds = ☐ + ☐ + ☐ + ☐ + ☐ + ☐ + ☐ + ☐ + ☐ + ☐ = ☐

▲ Fill in the spaces. These sums show how ones, tens, hundreds and thousands are connected.

The human number system is based on the idea of groups of tens. This system is called 'Base 10'. It's easy for humans to arrange their numbers in this way, because they only have ten fingers.

600 + 700 = 1300

800 + 900 =

1300 + 300 =

1000 + 900 =

900 + 900 =

700 + 800 =

◀ Space travel involves huge numbers! Work out these sums and write the answers in digits, then say them to someone else in words. For example, 1300 is 'one thousand three hundred'.

▼ Carry on this countdown towards zero.

100 tens = 1000 = one thousand
90 tens = 900 = _____
80 tens = ☐ = _____
☐ tens = ☐ = _____
☐ tens = ☐ = _____
☐ tens = ☐ = _____
☐ tens = ☐ = _____
☐ tens = ☐ = _____
☐ tens = ☐ = _____
☐ tens = ☐ = _____

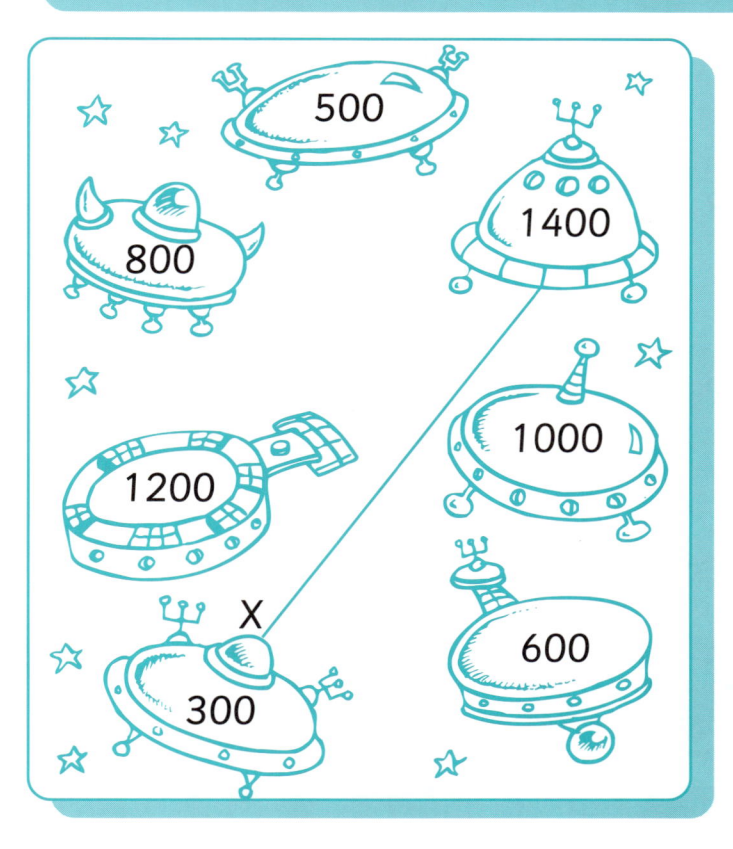

To find the 'hidden star', Zoth has to fly to all the space stations in order. Show his route. Start at X.

Space stations: 500, 800, 1400, 1200, 1000, X, 300, 600

When you finish this step put a sticker here!

Dear Parent or Carer

In our number system, ten ones make one ten (10), ten tens make one hundred (100), ten hundreds make one thousand (1000) and so on. Using this system (known as 'Base 10'), we can write any number using the symbols from 0 to 9. With sums involving larger numbers, check that your child is able to calculate using digits **and** to say the answers correctly in words. Answers on page 30.

Step 3

Adding 9 and 99

This step will help you to learn what happens to numbers when you add 9 or 99 to them.

Adding 10 is easy, but adding 9 is much harder.

Here's a quick way! Adding 9 is the same as adding 10 and taking away 1.

Keep adding 9 to each of these numbers. Can you see what is happening to the units digit?

2 →+9→ ☐ →+9→ ☐ →+9→ ☐ →+9→ ☐ →+9→ ☐ →+9→ ☐

5 →+9→ ☐ →+9→ ☐ →+9→ ☐ →+9→ ☐ →+9→ ☐ →+9→ ☐

8 →+9→ ☐ →+9→ ☐ →+9→ ☐ →+9→ ☐ →+9→ ☐ →+9→ ☐

Think about what happens to a number when you add 99. Work out these sums on paper or in your head, then check with a calculator.

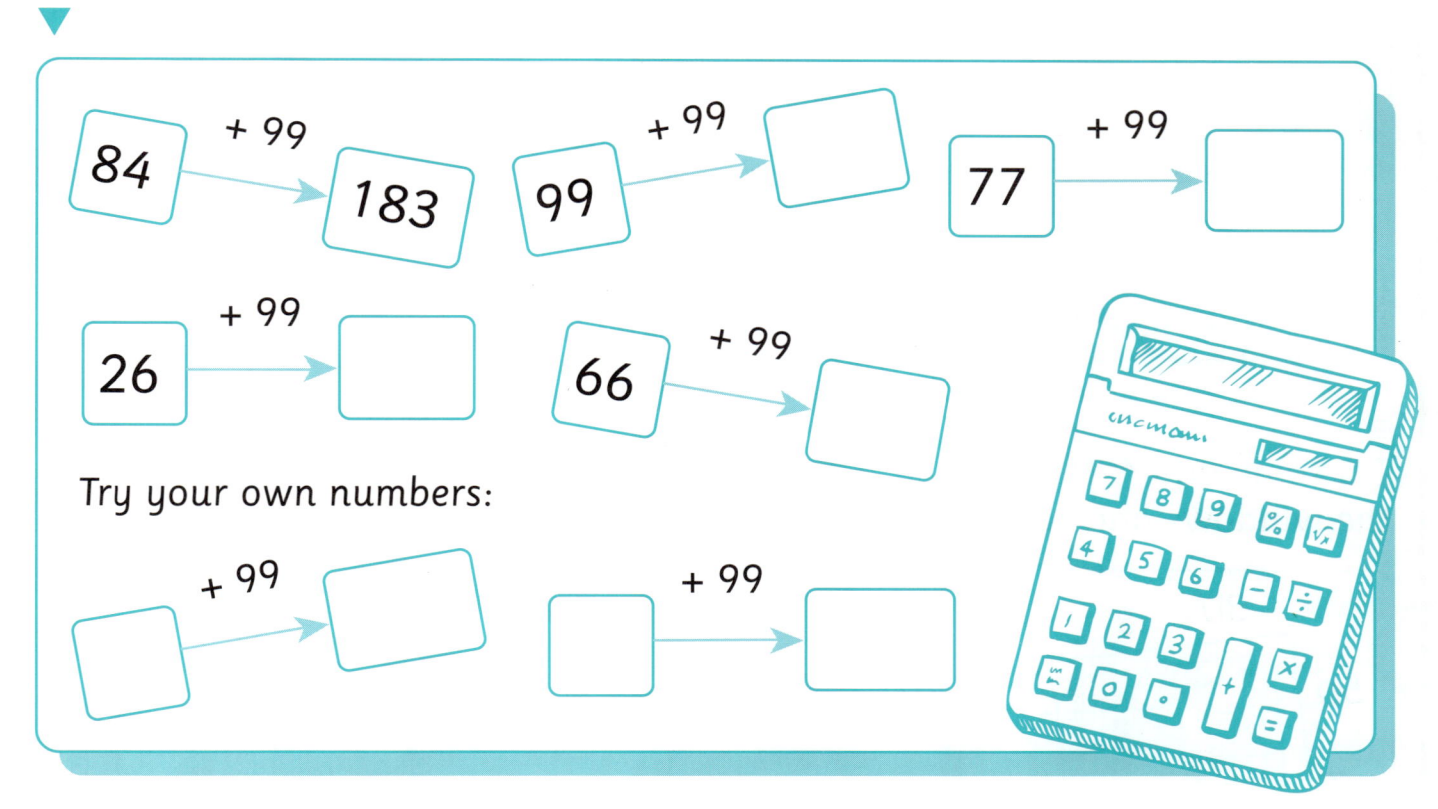

84 +99→ 183   99 +99→ ☐   77 +99→ ☐

26 +99→ ☐   66 +99→ ☐

Try your own numbers:

☐ +99→ ☐   ☐ +99→ ☐

Look at this 'Add 99' track. Can you see a pattern in the numbers? Use it to fill in the rest of the track.

0 | 99 | 198 | 297 | ☐ | ☐ | ☐ | ☐ | ☐ | ☐

Times tables are a quick way of adding a set of a number. For example, 3 × 9 is the same as 9 + 9 + 9.

Dear Parent or Carer

Knowing 'number tricks' or patterns for calculation can be very useful. Adding 9 to each counting number (12 + 9, 13 + 9 etc) forms an obvious pattern because it is 1 less than adding 10, and so the ones (units) digit in the answer goes down by one each time. Answers on page 30.

When you finish this step put a sticker here!

Step 4: Adding tens and ones

This step will help you to add two-digit numbers together.

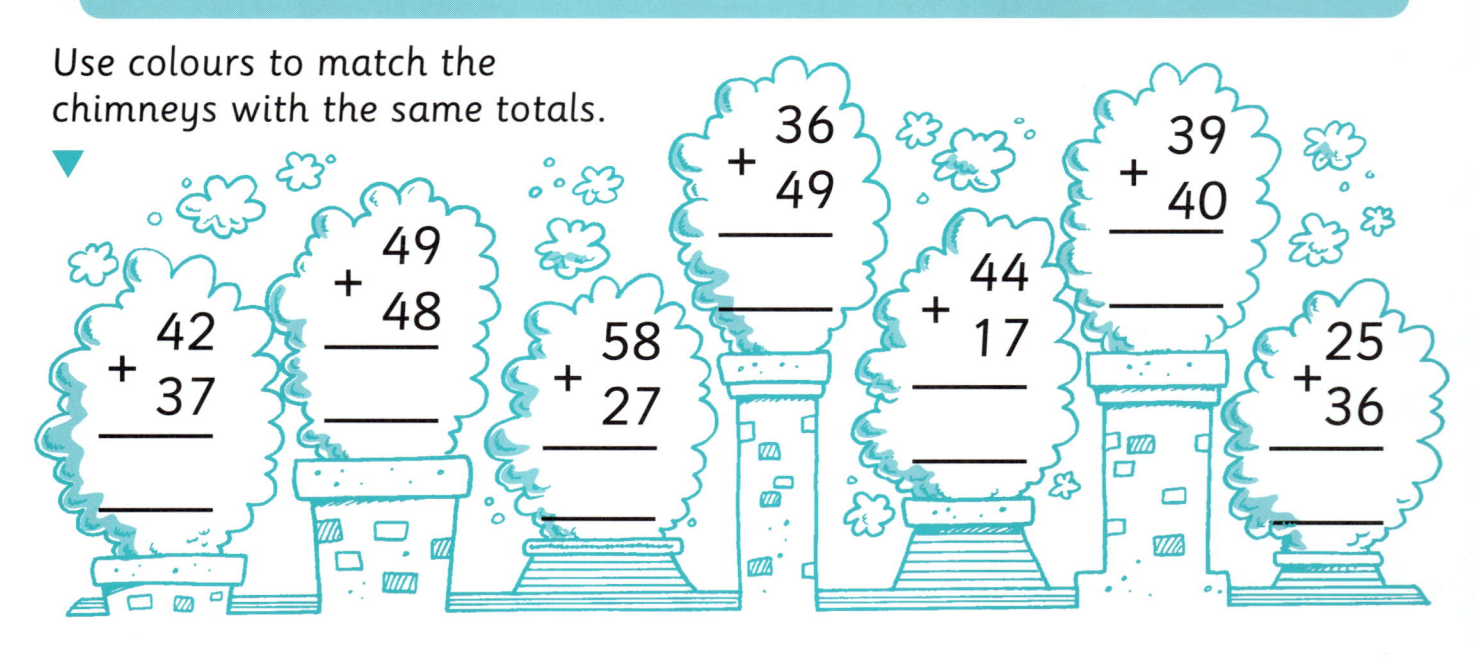

You can add two-digit numbers together using a window:
42 + 39 → 70 + 11 = 81

```
       40    2
   30 ┌──┬──┐
      │70│  │
      ├──┼──┤
    9 │  │11│
      └──┴──┘
```

Try some others for yourself. Fill in the windows and complete the sums:

    30   8
50 ┌──┬──┐
 7 │ │ │
   │ │ │
   └──┴──┘
38 + 57 →
☐

    20   9
40 ┌──┬──┐
 8 │ │ │
   └──┴──┘
29 + 48 →
☐

    60   2
50 ┌──┬──┐
 5 │ │ │
   └──┴──┘
62 + 55 →
☐

    70   7
60 ┌──┬──┐
 9 │ │ │
   └──┴──┘
77 + 69 →
☐

Use colours to match the chimneys with the same totals.

  42   49   58   36   44   39   25
+ 37   + 48   + 27   + 49   + 17   + 40   + 36
 ___   ___   ___   ___   ___   ___   ___

Which chimney is the odd one out?

26	+	32	+	48	+	22
+		+		+		+
74	+	63	+	52	+	63
+		+		+		+
86	+	39	+	91	+	26
+		+		+		+
36	+	41	+	59	+	51
+		+		+		+
67	+	45	+	18	+	82

Remember to check that your answers are about right! For example, the answer to 38 + 57 should be about 40 + 60, which is 100.

◀ Colour in the pairs of bricks in this wall (linked by a + sign) that make 100. How many can you find? One pair has already been found for you.

This factory doubles the number you put in. Use colours to match the input and output numbers. One has been done for you.

IN: 42, 74, 66, 57, 38, 82

OUT: 132, 114, 84, 164, 148, 76

Now turn over

Park the six cars so that every row, column and diagonal adds up to 150. ▶

Cars: 35, 40, 45, 50, 55, 60

35	70	45
60	50	40
55	30	65

Code breaker:
c = 65, d = 32, e = 80, h = 56, i = 71, k = 49, l = 81, m = 87, r = 91, t = 68, u = 39, y = 51

Use the code breaker above to find a well-known saying in the answers to the sums below. ▼

t	h	i	r	d	t	i	m	e

$47 + 21 = 68$

$28 + 28 = 56$

$37 + 34 = 71$

$49 + 42 = 91$

$17 + 15 = 32$

$49 + 19 = 68$

$58 + 13 = 71$

$33 + 54 = 87$

$55 + 25 = 80$

Use these digits to make lots of different sums. Use all four digits every time.

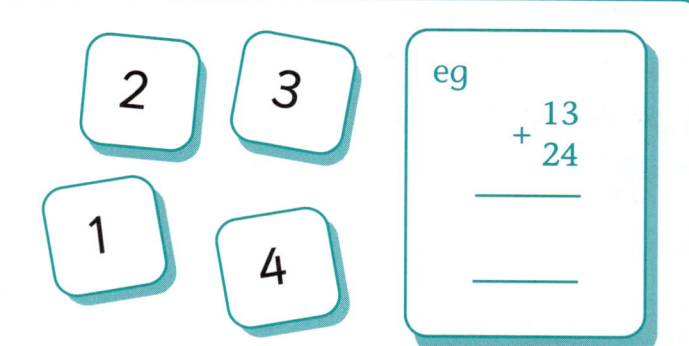

2 3

1 4

eg
13
$+24$
___

What is the largest total you can make? What is the smallest?

Do these sums, then use a calculator to check your answers.

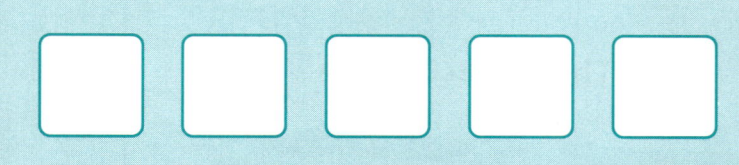

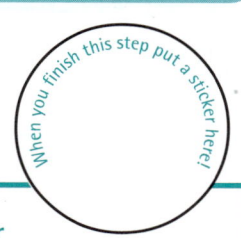

▼

99
$+99$

67
$+78$

56
$+65$

68
$+93$

62
$+19$

20
$+19$

38
$+27$

38
$+11$

26
$+25$

When you finish this step put a sticker here!

Dear Parent or Carer

Encourage your child to learn the number bonds to 18 (from 1 + 1 to 9 + 9). He or she will need to know what to do when the answer is more than 9 (to 'carry' to the tens). With activities that are not presented in the form of traditional sums, don't be surprised if your child works out the tens first and then calculates the units. This is a natural method when working mentally, and is now taught in many schools. Answers on pages 30–31.

Step 5: Subtracting tens and ones

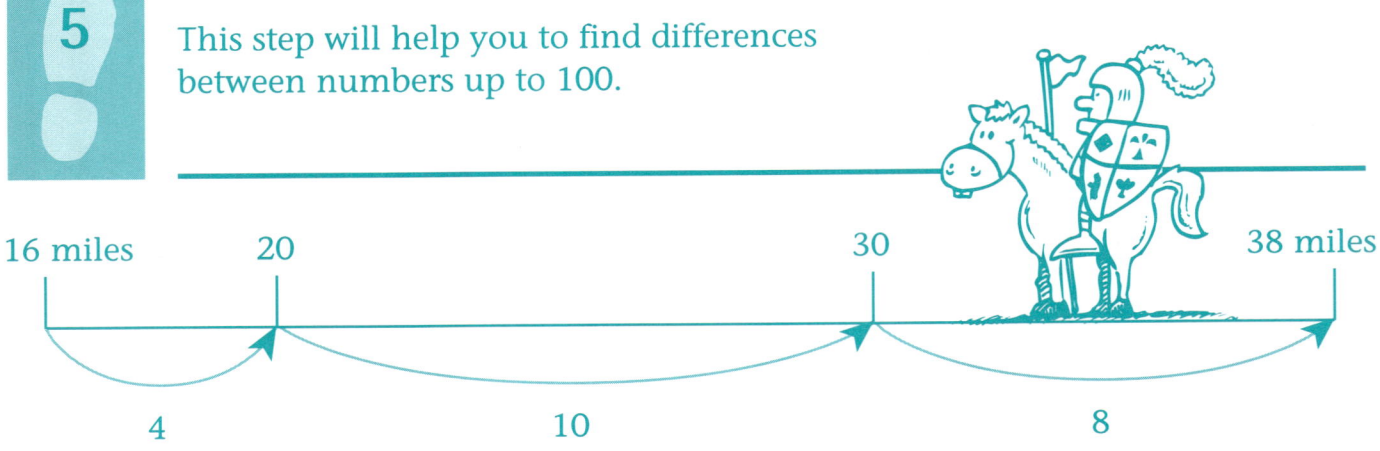

This step will help you to find differences between numbers up to 100.

16 miles — 20 — 30 — 38 miles
4   10   8

The difference between 16 miles and 38 miles from home is 4 + 10 + 8 = 22 miles.

Help the knight see how far from home he has to travel. Look at the example above, then calculate some distances for yourself.

23 miles — 70 miles
The difference is ☐

34 miles — 62 miles
The difference is ☐

15 miles — 91 miles
The difference is ☐

Make your own difference problem.

The difference is ☐

12

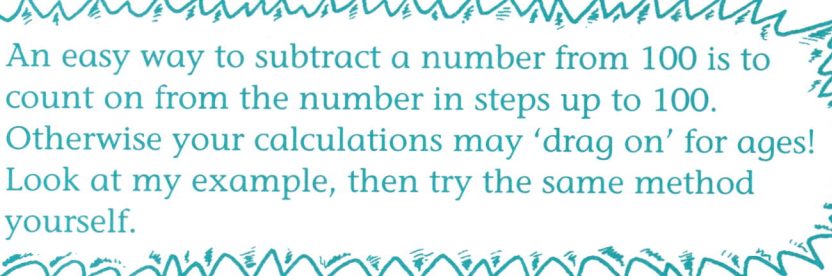

An easy way to subtract a number from 100 is to count on from the number in steps up to 100. Otherwise your calculations may 'drag on' for ages! Look at my example, then try the same method yourself.

```
  100
-  32
_____
    8 (makes 40)
   60 (makes 100)
_____
   68
```

```
  100
-  84
_____
```

```
  100
-  63
_____
```

```
  100
-  25
_____
```

```
  100
-  19
_____
```

```
  100
-  36
_____
```

```
  100
-  17
_____
```

```
  100
-  58
_____
```

```
  100
-  77
_____
```

```
  100
-  44
_____
```

Don't forget to check your answers by **adding**.
If 100 − 32 = 68
then 68 + 32 must be 100.

Now turn over

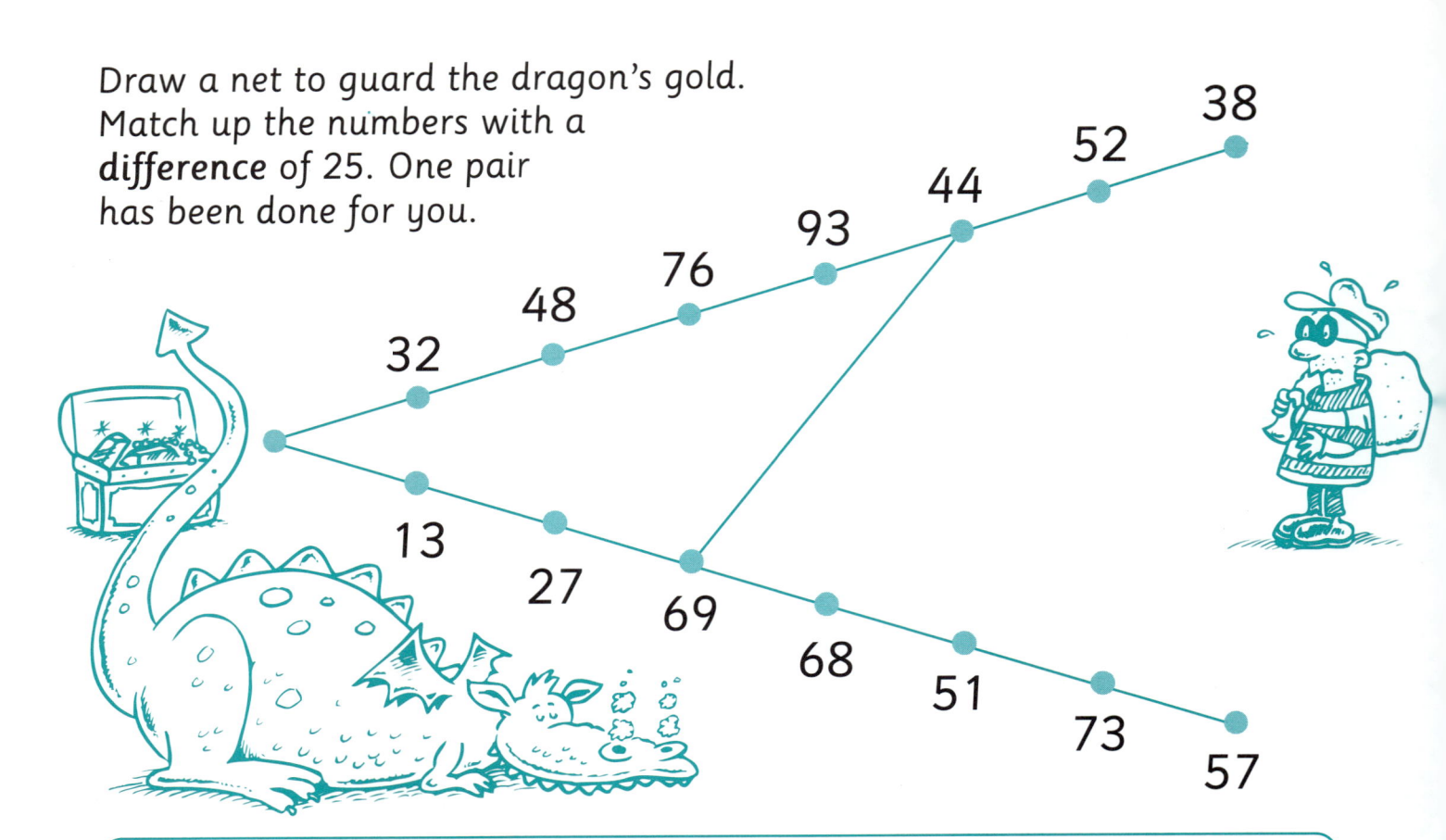

Draw a net to guard the dragon's gold. Match up the numbers with a **difference** of 25. One pair has been done for you.

This knight rides from one number to another. Fill in the table for the knight's different journeys. One blank has been filled in for you.

Start number — Finish number

Start number	Journey	Finish number
32	24	56
43		68
24		79
38		57
	48	99

− _ _ _ _	− _ _ _ _
1 1	1 8

− _ _ _ _	− _ _ _ _
2 9	

− _ _ _ _	− _ _ _ _
_ _	_ _

1 2 3 4

Use all four of these shutters to make each of the three answers shown above. ▲

Can you think of any other combinations? Show them in the last three sets of windows above. What answers do they make?

Work out these three subtractions in your head. Which key leads to the correct answer? ▼

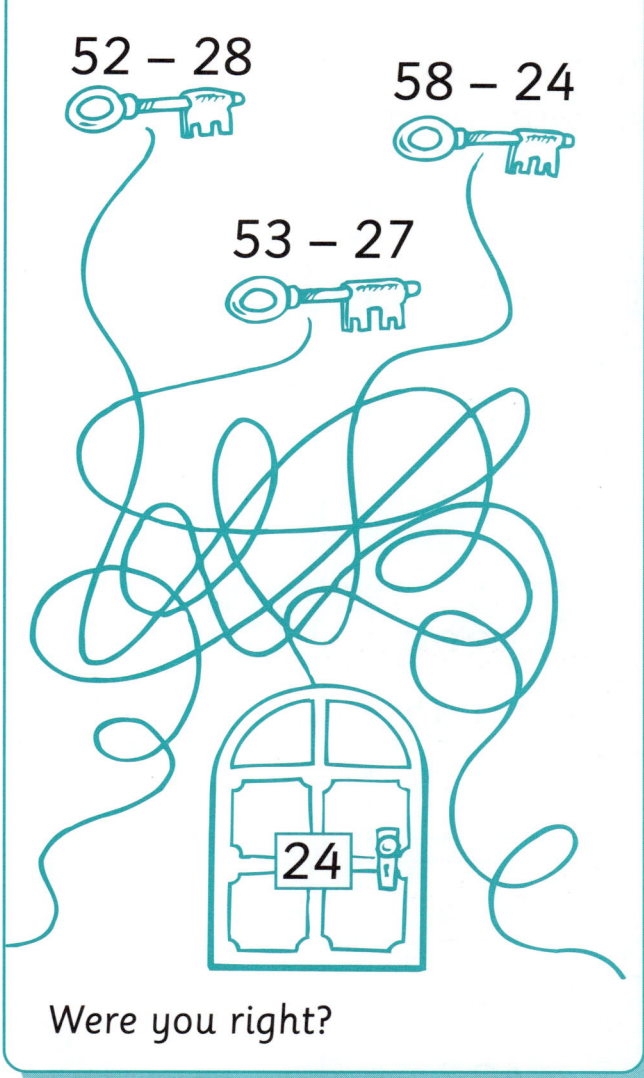

52 − 28   58 − 24

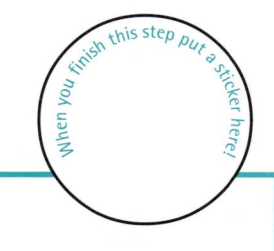

53 − 27

24

Were you right?

When you finish this step put a sticker here!

Dear Parent or Carer

Your child needs to be able to see subtraction in two ways:
- finding the **difference between** two amounts (eg 25 is 3 more than 22);
- taking one number **away from** another number (eg 25 take away 22 is 3).

If you are doing traditional subtraction sums with your child, try to work with the methods that your child is familiar with from school. Answers on page 31.

Step 6: Adding hundreds, tens and ones

This step will help you to practise adding numbers with totals up to 1000.

This floor has some tiles missing. Work out all the sums and write the answers in the appropriate places.

- a) 234 + 143
- j) 536 + 367
- f) 639 + 288
- i) 379 + 188
- d) 286 + 275
- h) 283 + 249
- m) 399 + 199
- b) 382 + 121
- e) 238 + 437
- c) 46 + 23
- g) 99 + 98
- k) 36 + 59
- l) 139 + 150

If two different numbers clash in any of the spaces, check your sums!

Astronomical numbers

A two-player game of strategy and luck

Cut out the two game boards and the 12 number tiles.
- Each player needs one board and one set of numbers 1–6.
- Take turns to roll a dice. Place the matching number tile on any one of the four spaces. It cannot then be moved.
- Take further turns until both players have occupied all four spaces on their game boards.
- If you roll a number you have already used, roll again until you get an unused number tile.
- The winner is the player who has made the largest four-digit number.

Variations
1. Play for the lowest score, or the nearest to a target total such as 3000.
2. Play the best of several rounds.

Let's Learn at Home © Scholastic Ltd 1998

Fraction pieces – activities and game

Activity 1: Can you find different ways of making up a whole circle? For example:
$\frac{1}{2} + \frac{1}{4} + \frac{1}{8} + \frac{1}{8}$.

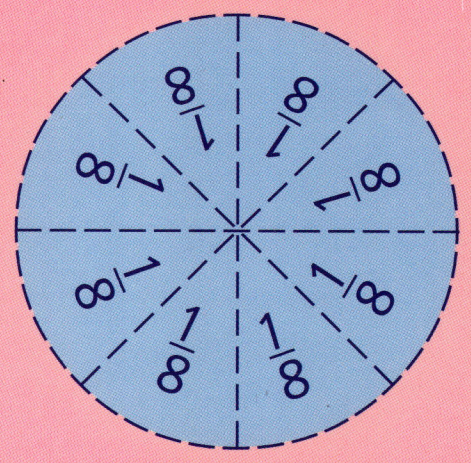

Activity 2: Use the pieces to compare the fractions. For example, how many $\frac{1}{8}$s make $\frac{3}{4}$?

✂ Cut along the dotted lines.

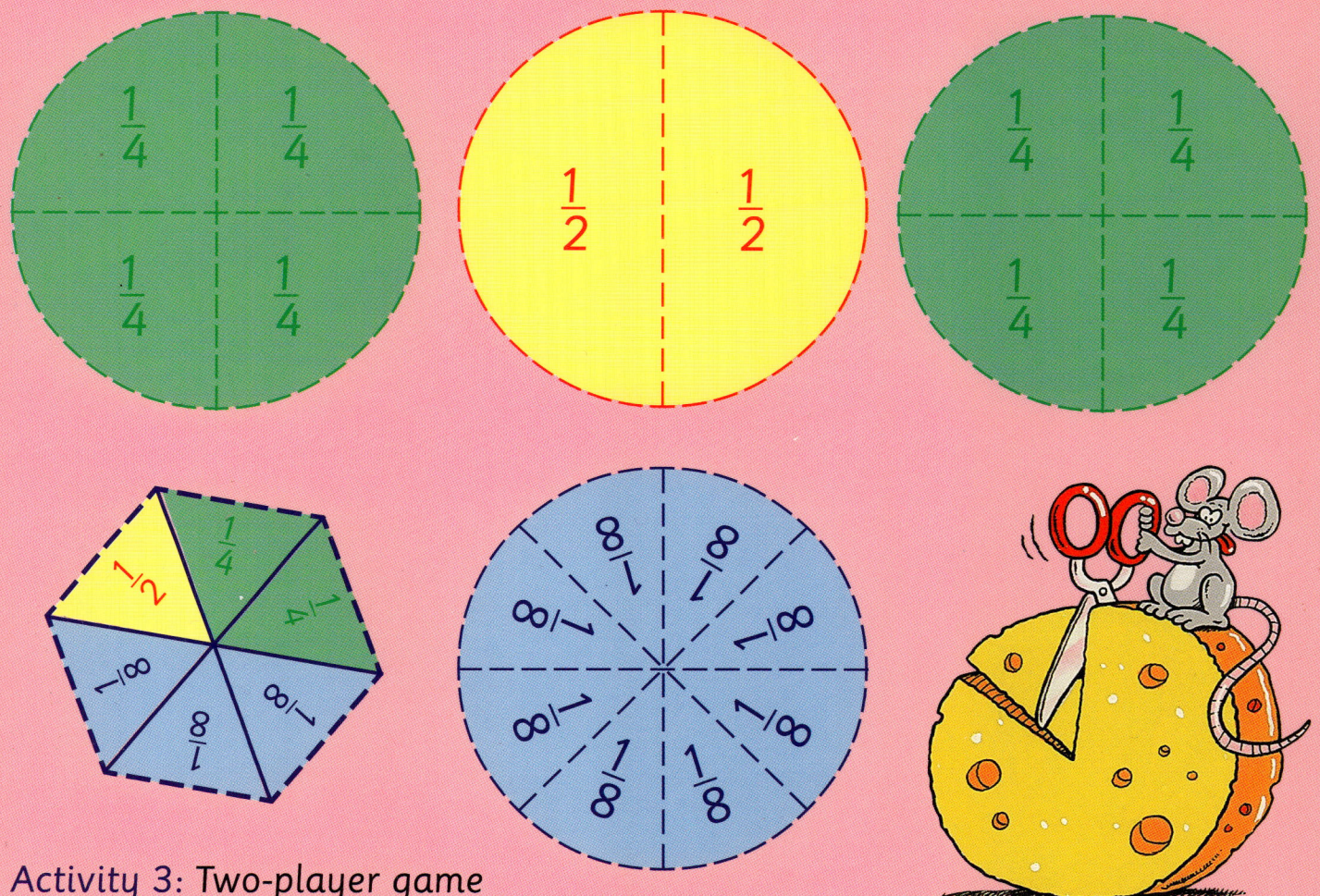

Activity 3: Two-player game
You need the spinner for this game.
- Take turns to spin a number and collect the matching fraction piece.
- Try to build up your collection of pieces to form 2 whole units. You must get the right final piece to win the game.
- If you spin a fraction for which all of the pieces have been taken, you cannot collect a piece – you will have to wait until your next turn and roll again.

Pair up the dancing partners that add up to 1000. One pair has been done for you.
Who will be left out when the music starts?

864 666 288 136 572 767
233 428 712 214
429 786 455 571 545

Use these numbers to make lots of different sums. Use all six numbers every time.

1 2 3 4 5 6

eg
```
  134
+ 256
-----
  390
```

What is the largest total you can make?

Starting with 123, +111 each step.

Carry on this number sequence.
Can you see a pattern in the answers?

Build these number towers by adding the numbers at the base of each set. The first one has been done for you.

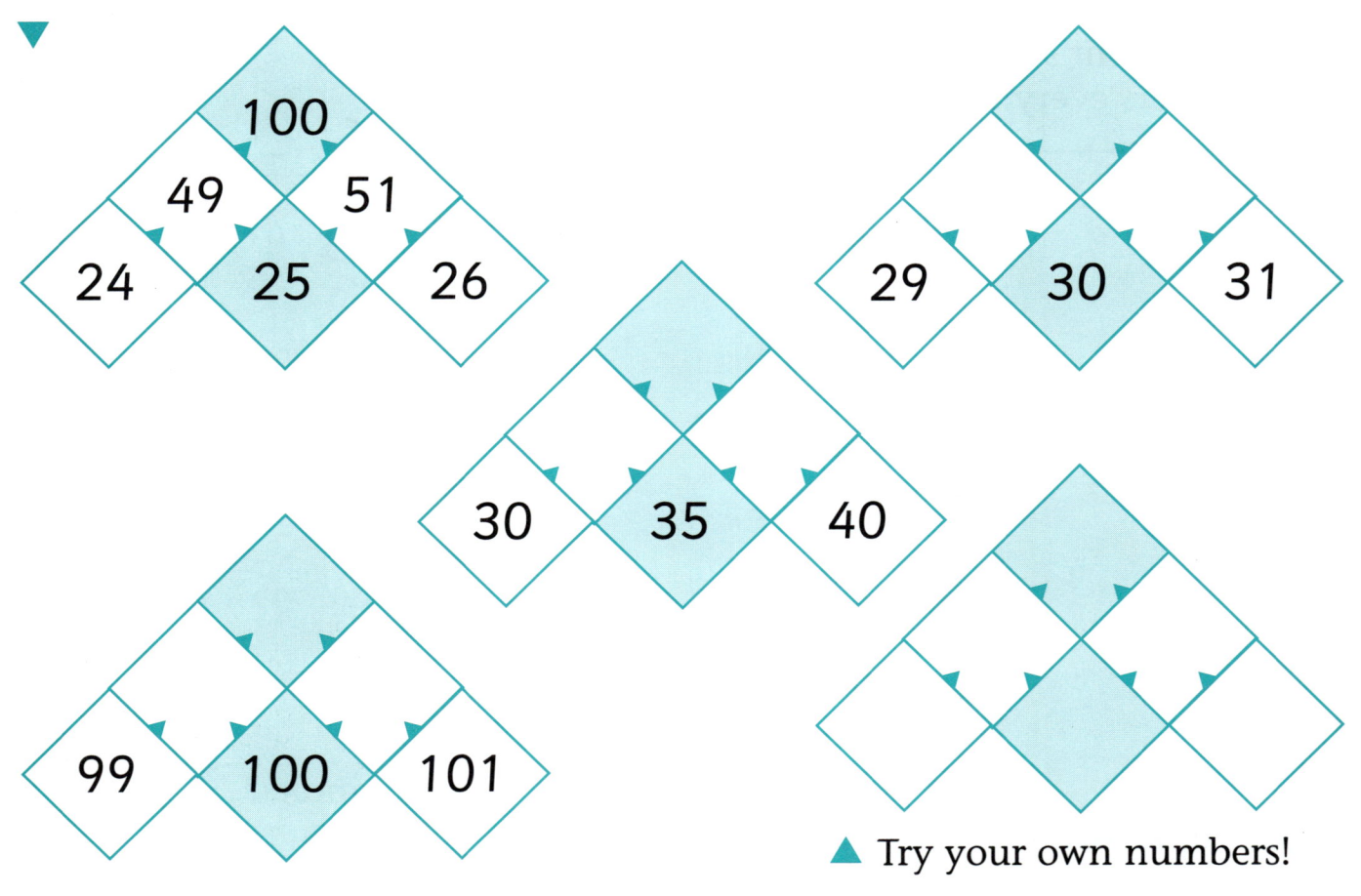

100
49 51
24 25 26

29 30 31

30 35 40

99 100 101

Try your own numbers!

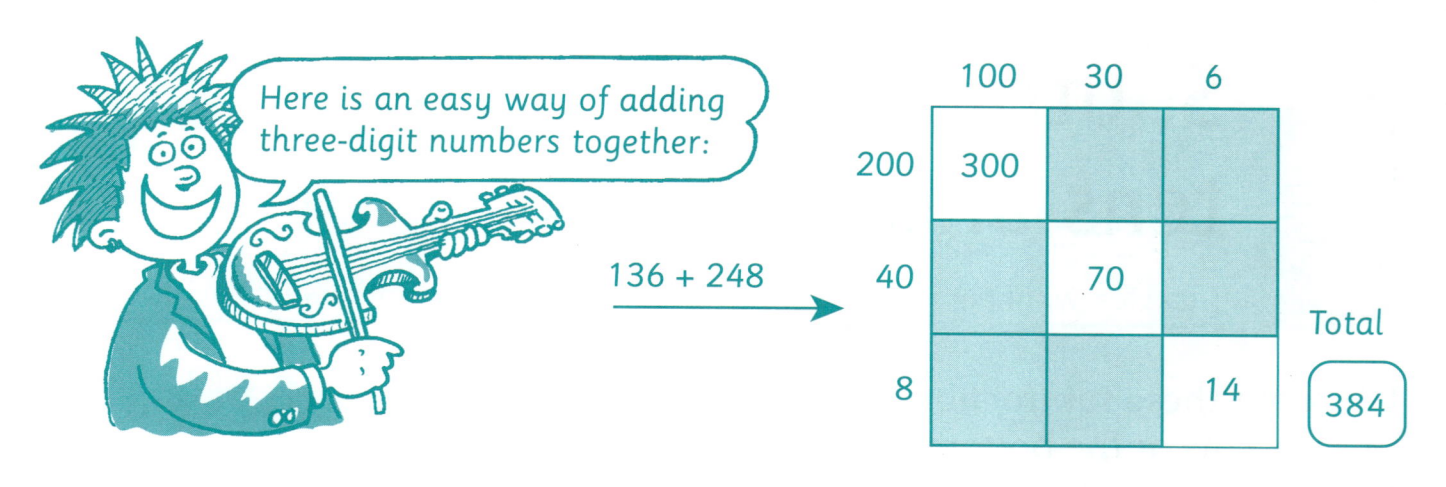

Here is an easy way of adding three-digit numbers together:

136 + 248 →

	100	30	6
200	300		
40		70	
8			14

Total: 384

Now try doing these sums in the same way: ▼

258 + 417

Total

483 + 289

Total

199 + 298

Total

Make sure you don't miss any steps!

When you finish this step put a sticker here!

Dear Parent or Carer

This step develops the content of Steps 1 to 4 with larger numbers (up to 1000). It is important for your child to understand the idea of 'place value' – that is, the way that the value of a digit depends on its place. For example, in the number 564 the 6 has a value of 60 because it is in the 'tens' place. Some of the activities in this step also test your child's ability to work with numbers presented in unfamiliar ways. The pull-out game 'Astronomical numbers' will help to reinforce these ideas. Answers on pages 31–32.

Step 7: Subtracting hundreds, tens and ones

This step will help you to practise subtracting with numbers up to 1000.

Work out these subtraction problems and shade in the answer bats at the bottom of the page. One bat has flown onto the wrong page. Which one is it?

▼

137 − 22	189 − 37	168 − 62	145 − 35	160 − 38	190 − 43
115					

132 − 33	178 − 89	285 − 153	475 − 235	632 − 418	583 − 327

Answers

240   187   132   152
256   106   89   115
99   122   110   214   147

Here is a quick way of working out differences:

Take it to the bridge!

$2 + 30 + 6 = 38$

68 70   100   106

2   30   6

Now work out these differences for yourself. Remember to 'bridge' across 100 every time.

55   100   120

33   100   126

27   100   116

Make up another example:

                                        100

Subtracting from 1000 isn't so hard if you Count on! Look at this example, then use the same method to work out the subtractions.

```
 1000
- 746
------
    4   (makes 750)
   50   (makes 800)
  200   (makes 1000)
------
  254
```

1000
− 626

1000
− 458

1000
− 233

1000
− 226

1000
− 185

1000
− 101

1000
− 92

1000
− 347

Use a calculator to check your answers.

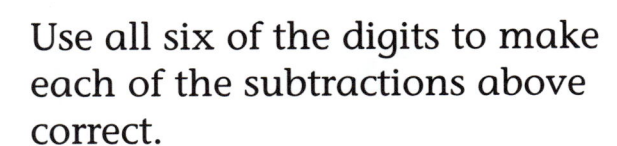

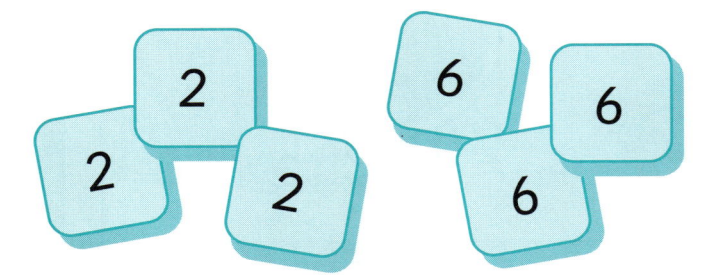

Two vampires have a total age of 1000 years. The difference between their ages is 500 years. How old are they? ▶

☐ + ☐ = 1000

☐ − ☐ = 500

```
  ☐ ☐ ☐           ☐ ☐ ☐
−                −
  ☐ ☐ ☐           ☐ ☐ ☐
  ─────           ─────
  4 4 4           3 6 4


  ☐ ☐ ☐           ☐ ☐ ☐
−                −
  ☐ ☐ ☐           ☐ ☐ ☐
  ─────           ─────
      4           3 5 6
```

▲ Use all six of the digits to make each of the subtractions above correct.

2 2 2   6 6 6

Dear Parent or Carer

This step deals with subtracting numbers up to and including 1000. Although these activities may appear demanding, they are basically extensions (with larger numbers) of the activities in Steps 5 and 7. This step will also help to emphasise the close link between addition and subtraction. Answers on page 32.

When you finish this step put a sticker here!

Step 8: Solving problems using addition and subtraction

This step will help you to think about maths in real life.

148 boys are lost in a forest. There are 23 more girls than boys lost in the forest. How many children are lost in the forest altogether?

Answer:

A witch's brew is made up of beetles and mice. Hepzibah the witch used 7 creatures with a total of 36 legs.

How many 🪲 and how many 🐭 did I use?

Hepzibah used ☐ 🪲

and ☐ 🐭

Place these five rats to make the sum on the left correct.

```
  [ ]   [ ]   [ ]
+     [ ]   [ ]
―――――――――――――――
  2     8     1
```

Rats numbered: 2, 3, 4, 5, 6

These two goblins look the same, but one is 30 years older than the other. Between them, they are 1000 years old. How old are they?

[ ] + [ ] = 1000

[ ] − [ ] = 30

The two ages are [ ] years and [ ] years

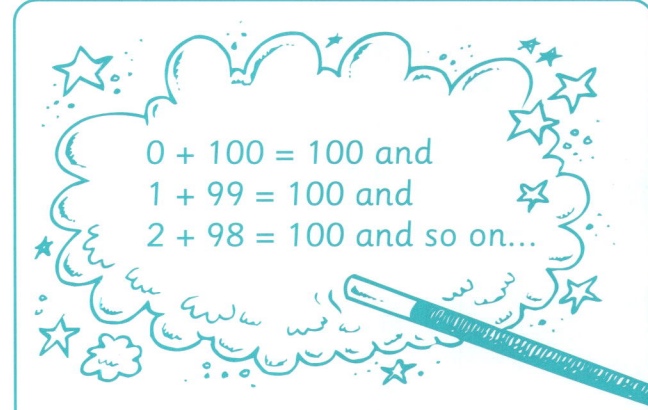

---

0 + 100 = 100 and
1 + 99 = 100 and
2 + 98 = 100 and so on…

How many ways are there of making 100 by adding two whole numbers?

There are [ ] ways.

Dear Parent or Carer

Maths often seems harder when we cannot see an obvious method for dealing with a problem. If your child finds these activities difficult, remind him or her that there is no 'right' way of finding the answers. 'Trial and error' (sometimes called 'trial and improvement') is a useful approach to some of these tasks, so don't discourage it as a method. Answers on page 32.

Step 9 Working with fractions

This step will help you to find and add together fractions of a whole shape and fractions of a number.

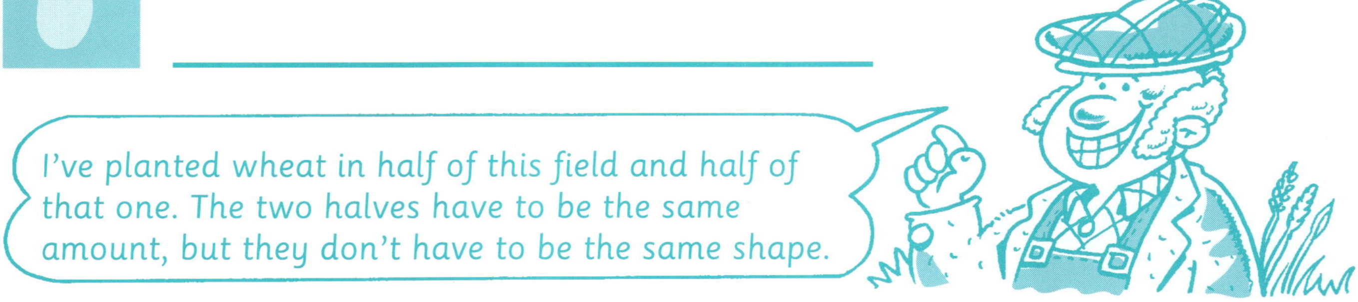

I've planted wheat in half of this field and half of that one. The two halves have to be the same amount, but they don't have to be the same shape.

Find some different ways of shading in half of each field. A few have already been done for you. ▼

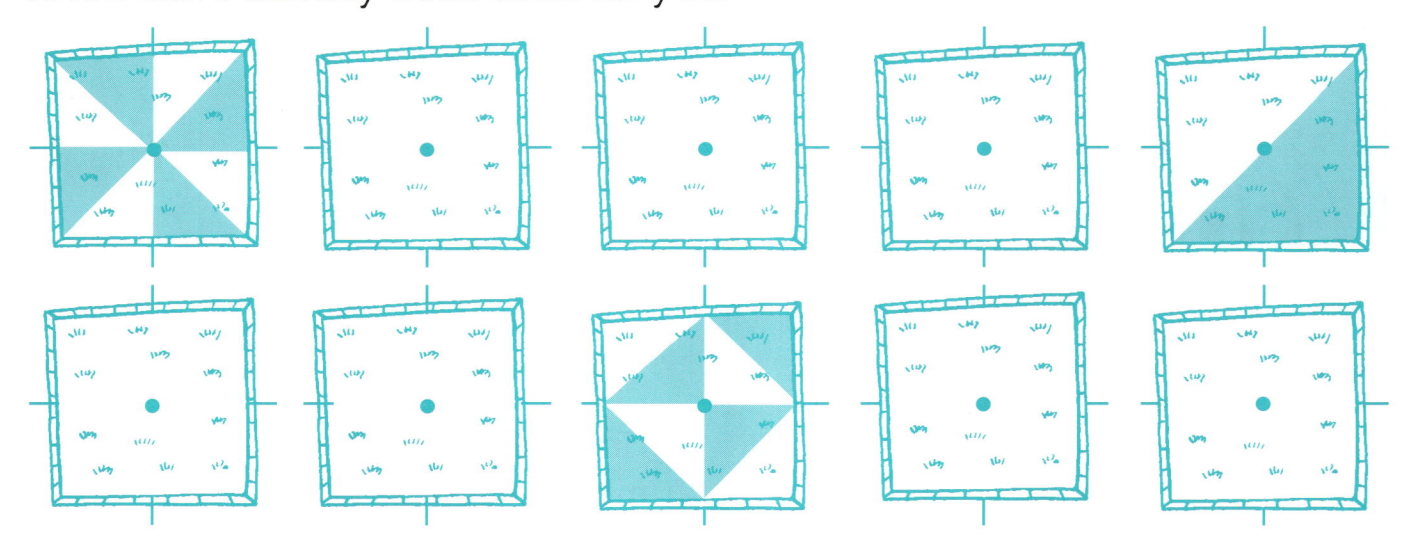

Shade $\frac{1}{2}$ the sheep.

$\frac{1}{2}$ of 8 = 4

Shade $\frac{1}{4}$ of the goats.

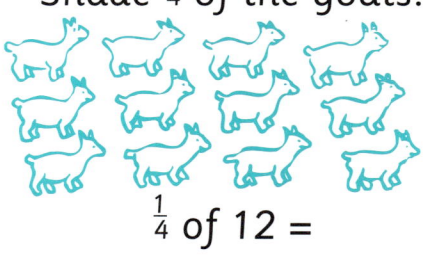

$\frac{1}{4}$ of 12 =

Shade $\frac{1}{3}$ of the rabbits.

$\frac{1}{3}$ of 6 =

Shade $\frac{1}{4}$ of the cows.

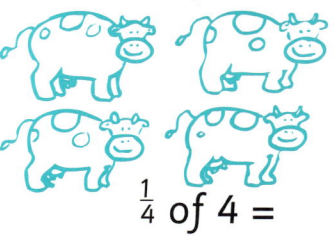

$\frac{1}{4}$ of 4 =

If you need to find ¾ of a number, work out what ¼ of that number is. Then add three ¼s together. For example, ¼ of 12 is 3 and 3 + 3 + 3 = 9, so ¾ of 12 is 9.

Shade $\frac{3}{4}$ of the hens.

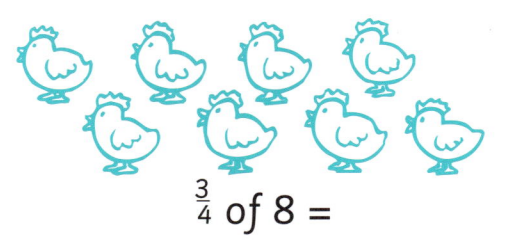

$\frac{3}{4}$ of 8 =

Shade $\frac{2}{3}$ of the ducks.

$\frac{2}{3}$ of 9 =

This number line is marked in 'jumps' of one quarter. Use the number line to help you work out the sums below. The first one has been done for you. ▼

0   ¼   ½   ¾   1   1¼   1½   1¾   2   2¼   2½   2¾   3

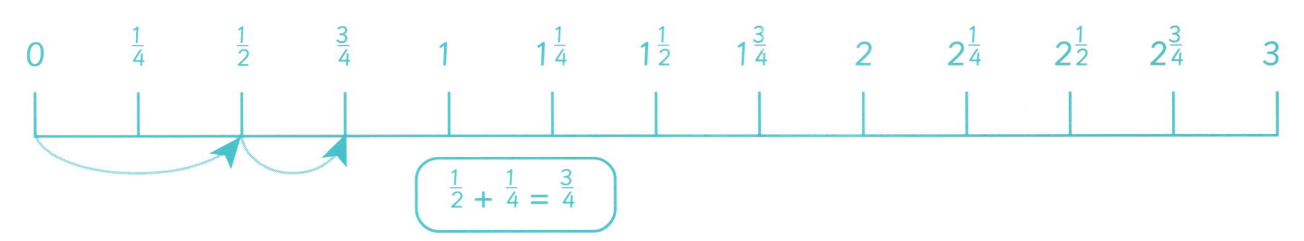

$\frac{1}{2} + \frac{1}{4} = \frac{3}{4}$

$\frac{1}{2} + \frac{1}{4} = \boxed{\frac{3}{4}}$ $\frac{1}{4} + \frac{3}{4} = \boxed{}$ $\frac{1}{4} + \frac{1}{2} = \boxed{}$

$\frac{1}{2} + \frac{3}{4} = \boxed{}$ $\frac{3}{4} + 1\frac{1}{4} = \boxed{}$ $\frac{3}{4} + \frac{3}{4} = \boxed{}$

24 geese flew South for the winter. One third of them were male. How many female geese flew South?

When you finish this step put a sticker here!

Dear Parent or Carer

This step begins with work on fractions of a shape. Note that there is more than one way to divide an area in half. The rest of the activities in this step deal with fractions of a number. Your child needs to understand both of these ways of looking at fractions. You might like to play the fraction game (see the pull-out) with your child in order to help him or her become familiar with the links between common fractions. Answers on page 32.

Step 10: Adding decimals

This step will help you to recognise decimals and add them together.

Decimals are another – often neater – way of writing fractions. As well as writing whole numbers as hundreds, tens and units, we can write parts of numbers as tenths, hundredths and so on. The decimal point shows where the fraction would start. For example:

143.47 = $100 + 40 + 3 + \frac{4}{10} + \frac{7}{100}$

↑ decimal point

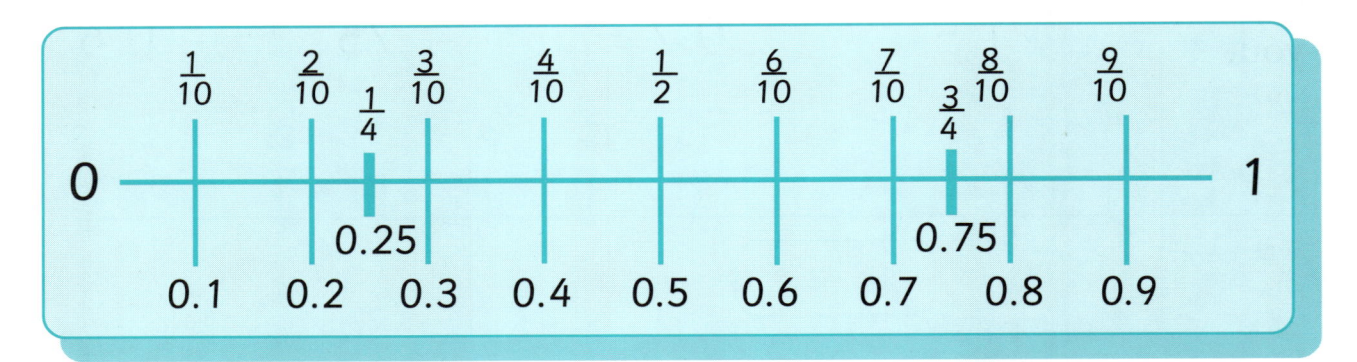

Number line from 0 to 1 showing: $\frac{1}{10}$ (0.1), $\frac{2}{10}$ (0.2), $\frac{1}{4}$ (0.25), $\frac{3}{10}$ (0.3), $\frac{4}{10}$ (0.4), $\frac{1}{2}$ (0.5), $\frac{6}{10}$ (0.6), $\frac{7}{10}$ (0.7), $\frac{3}{4}$ (0.75), $\frac{8}{10}$ (0.8), $\frac{9}{10}$ (0.9)

Use the number line to shade in the correct fraction of each pizza. ▲

0.3

0.5

0.9

0.75

0.5

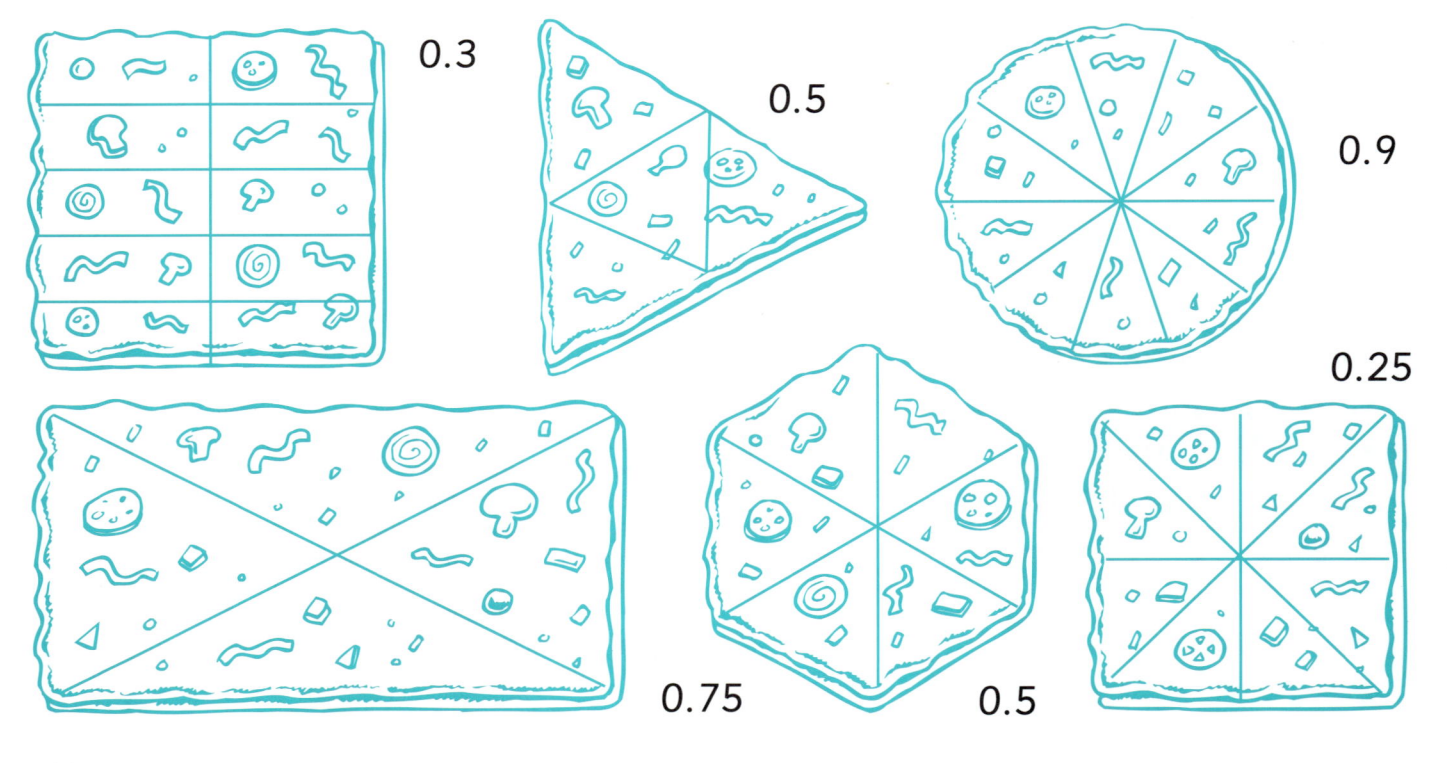

0.25

0.5 + 0.5 = $\frac{1}{2}$ + $\frac{1}{2}$ = 1

0.25 + 0.5 = ☐ + ☐ = ☐

0.5 + 0.75 = ☐ + ☐ = ☐

0.75 + 0.75 = ☐ + ☐ = ☐

Solve these problems for yourself.

```
  0.7        0.5        0.4       1.75       0.8
+ 0.5      + 1.5      + 0.7     + 1.75     + 0.6
─────      ─────      ─────     ──────     ─────


                        0.25       0.9       0.25
                      + 0.25     + 0.9     + 0.75
                      ──────     ─────     ──────
```

Don't forget to use the decimal point in your answers to these sums. It's really not so different from adding up with whole numbers. Decimals and fractions are different ways of making the same thing. Like pasta shells and spaghetti!

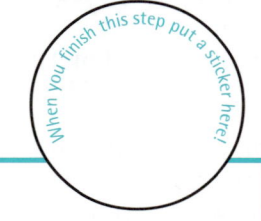

When you finish this step put a sticker here!

Dear Parent or Carer

This step deals with simple decimals (teachers call these 'decimal fractions', since whole numbers in our number system are 'decimal' too) and how to add them together. It may be helpful to discuss with your child the ways that decimals are used in everyday life – for example, money (one pound and 65p is written as £1.65) and calculator arithmetic (to find ¼ of 25, key in 25 ÷ 4 and the answer will be displayed as 6.25). Make sure that your child understands the use of the decimal point. Answers on page 32.

Parents' pages

👣 Step 1 Adding tens

Page 2:
3 tens = 10+10+10=30
4 tens = 10+10+10+10= 40
5 tens = 10+10+10+10+10=50
6 tens = 10+10+10+10+10+10=60
7 tens = 10+10+10+10+10+10+10=70
8 tens = 10+10+10+10+10+10+10+10=80
9 tens = 10+10+10+10+10+10+10+10+10=90
10 tens = 10+10+10+10+10+10+10+10+10+10=100

	40	
30	20	60
	50	

	20	
30	40	50
	60	

	40	
20	60	50
	30	

(The numbers in the horizontal and vertical arms of the crosses could be reversed or swapped over.)

Page 3:

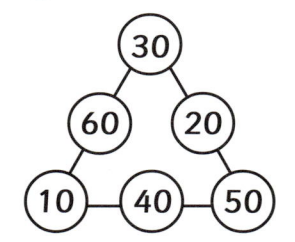

```
      30
    60  20
  10  40  50
```

(Alternatively, 10 or 50 could go at the top.)

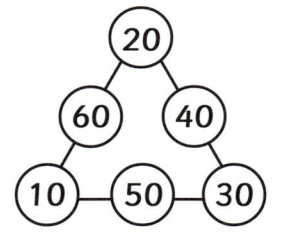

```
      20
    60  40
  10  50  30
```

For a total of 90 on each side.

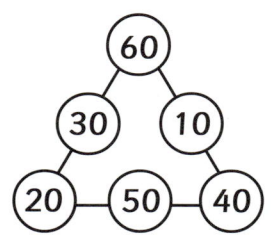

```
      60
    30  10
  20  50  40
```

For a total of 110 on each side.

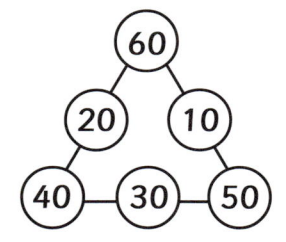

```
      60
    20  10
  40  30  50
```

For a total of 120 on each side.

20 + 20 = 40; 30 + 30 = 60; 40 + 40 = 80; 50 + 50 = 100; 60 + 60 = 120; 70 + 70 = 140; 80 + 80 = 160; 90 + 90 = 180.
The answers are even numbers. They increase by two 10s each time.

👣 Step 2 Adding hundreds

Page 4: Ten tens = 10 + 10 + 10 + 10 + 10 + 10 + 10 + 10 + 10 + 10 = 100; ten hundreds = 100 + 100 + 100 +100 +100 +100 +100 +100 +100 +100 = 1000.
1700, 1600, 1900, 1800, 1500.

Page 5:
90 tens = 900 = nine hundred
80 tens = 800 = eight hundred
70 tens = 700 = seven hundred
60 tens = 600 = six hundred
50 tens = 500 = five hundred
40 tens = 400 = four hundred
30 tens = 300 = three hundred
20 tens = 200 = two hundred
10 tens = 100 = one hundred

👣 Step 3 Adding 9 and 99

Page 6: 2 11 20 29 38 47
          5 14 23 32 41 50
          8 17 26 35 44 53
The units digit goes down by 1 each time.
Page 7: 99 → 198; 77 → 176; 26 → 125; 66 → 165.
396, 495, 594, 693, 792, 891, 990.

👣 Step 4 Adding tens and ones

Page 8: 38 + 57 → 80 + 15 = 95;
29 + 48 → 60 + 17 = 77; 62 + 55 → 110 + 7 = 117;
77 + 69 → 130 + 16 = 146.

42 + 37 = **79** = 39 + 40; 36 + 49 = **85** = 58 + 27; 49 + 48 = 97 (the odd one out); 44 + 17 = **61** = 25 + 36.

Page 9:

26	+	32	+	48	+	22
+		+		+		+
74	+	63	+	52	+	63
+		+		+		+
86	+	39	+	91	+	26
+		+		+		+
36	+	41	+	59	+	51
+		+		+		+
67	+	45	+	18	+	82

42 → 84, 74 → 148, 57 → 114, 38 → 76, 82 → 164.

Page 10:

```
        35    70    45
        60    50    40
        55    30    65
```
68 56 71 91 32   68 71 87 80   81 39 65 49 51
T H I R D   T I M E   L U C K Y

Page 11: Largest total is 73. Smallest total is 37. 198, 145, 121, 161.

Step 5 Subtracting tens and ones

Page 12: Your child should use the number line to jump to the nearest 10 or count on in 10s, then count on the remaining units. Thus from 23 to 70 is 7 + four 10s = 47; from 34 to 62 is 6 + two 10s + 2 = 28; from 15 to 91 is 5 + seven 10s + 1 = 76.

Page 13:

```
  100       100       100       100       100
 - 84      - 63      - 25      - 19      - 36
   6         7         5         1         4
  10        30        70        80        60
  16        37        75        81        64

  100       100       100       100
 - 17      - 58      - 77      - 44
   3         2         3         6
  80        40        20        50
  83        42        23        56
```

Page 14:

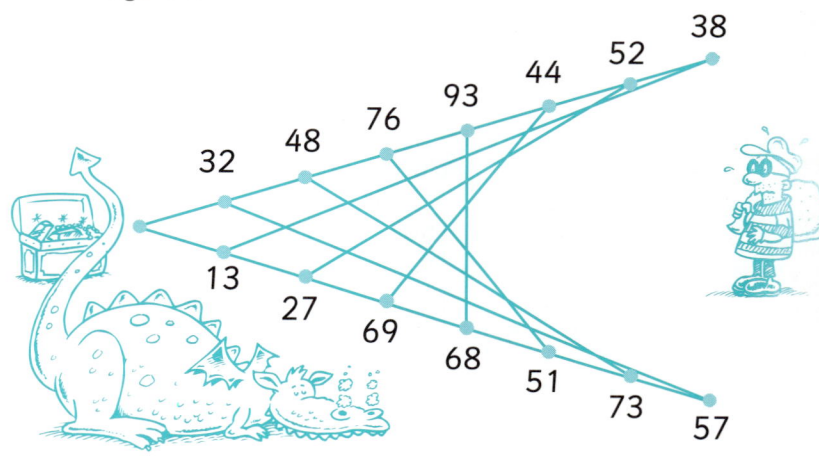

43 → 68 = 25; 24 → 79 = 55; 38 → 57 = 19;
51 → 99 = 48.
Page 15: 42 − 31 = 11 or 24 − 13 = 11; 32 − 14 = 18 or 41 − 23 = 18; 42 − 13 = 29.
52 − 28 leads to the door.

Step 6 Adding hundreds, tens and ones

Page 16: a 377, b 503, c 69, d 561, e 675, f 927, g 197, h 532, i 567, j 903, k 95; l 289, m 598.
Page 17: 214 → 786; 767 → 233; 545 → 455; 288 → 712; 136 → 864; 429 → 571; 428 → 572.
Number 666 is left out.
Many different sums can be made with the numbers, for example 234 + 156 = 390 and 523 + 416 = 939. The largest possible total is 1173.
Page 18: 123, 234, 345, 456, 567, 678, 789.
In this number sequence, the digit in each of the hundreds, tens and ones places goes up by 1 each time, so the last two digits in the first number are the first two digits of the next number.

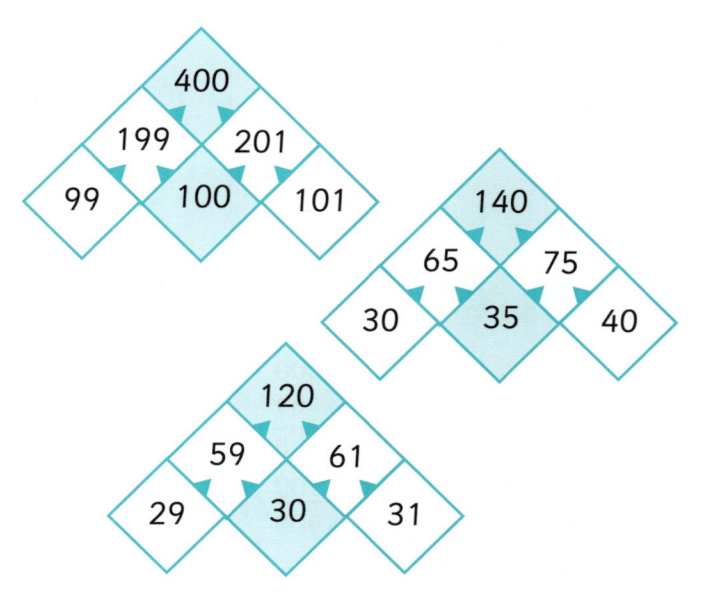

31

Page 19:

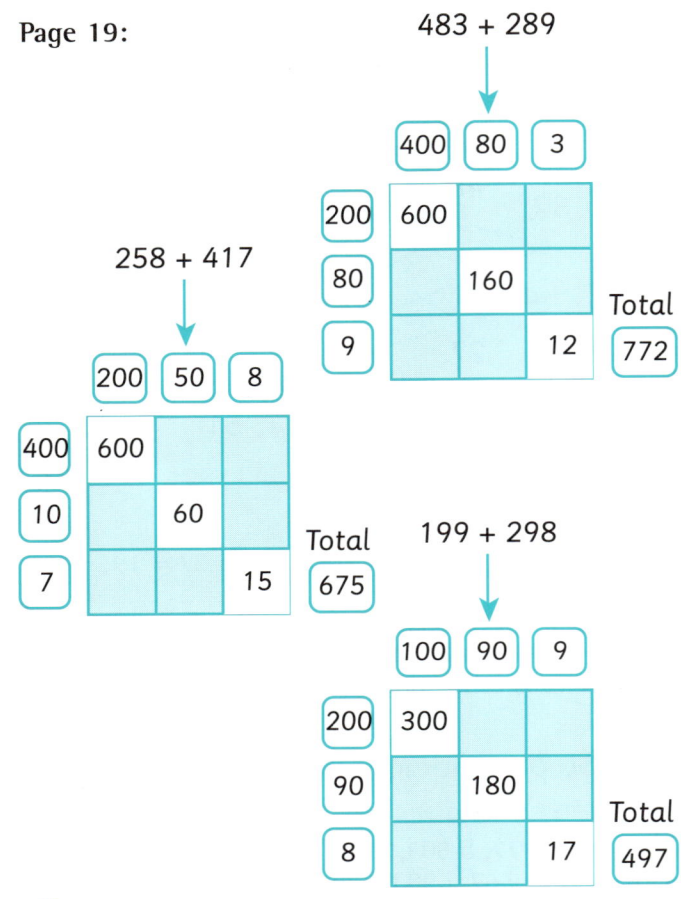

258 + 417

	200	50	8
400	600		
10		60	
7			15

Total 675

483 + 289

	400	80	3
200	600		
80		160	
9			12

Total 772

199 + 298

	100	90	9
200	300		
90		180	
8			17

Total 497

Step 7 Subtracting hundreds, tens and ones

Page 20: 152, 106, 110, 122, 147, 99, 89, 132, 240, 214, 256. The unused answer is 187.

Page 21: 5 + 40 + 20 = 65; 7 + 60 + 20 + 6 = 93; 3 + 70 + 10 + 6 = 89. Sometimes it is more convenient to count on to find a difference, as in these number line distances, than it is to do a subtraction in your head: to work out 106 − 68, it is easier to calculate that 68 + 32 + 6 = 106, so the difference between 68 and 106 is 38.

Page 22:

```
  1000      1000      1000      1000
-  626    -  458    -  233    -  226
     4         2         7         4
    70        40        60        70
   300       500       700       700
   374       542       767       774

  1000      1000      1000      1000
- 185     - 101     -  92     - 347
     5         9         8         3
    10        90       900        50
   800       800       908       600
   815       899                  653
```

Page 23: 750 years and 250 years.

```
  666       626       626  or  266       622
- 222     - 262     - 622     - 262     - 266
  444       364         4         4       356
```

Step 8 Solving problems using addition and subtraction

Page 24: there are 148 + 23 girls lost in the forest, so the total number of children lost in the forest is 148 + 148 + 23 = 319.
Hepzibah's brew has 4 beetles and 3 mice.

Page 25:

```
  2 3 5    or    2 4 6
+  4 6         +  3 5
  2 8 1          2 8 1
```

The two goblins are 515 and 485 years old. This answer can be found by reasoning that they must both be about 500 years old, so their ages should fall on either side of 500 years.
There are 51 ways to make 100 by adding a pair of whole numbers: from 0 + 100 to 50 + 50.

Step 9 Working with fractions

Page 26:
Three goats shaded: 1/4 of 12 = 3
Two rabbits shaded: 1/3 of 6 = 2
One cow shaded: 1/4 of 4 = 1

Page 27:
Six hens shaded: 3/4 of 8 = 6
Six ducks shaded: 2/3 of 9 = 6
1, 3/4, 1 1/4, 2, 1 1/2.
1/3 of 24 is 8, so the number of female geese flying South was 24 − 8 = 16.

Step 10 Adding decimals

Page 28:

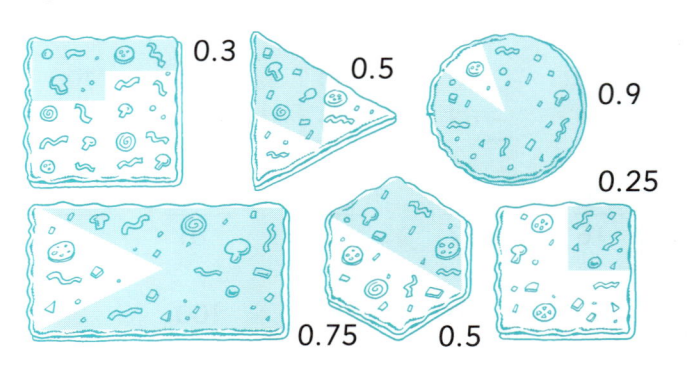

0.3, 0.5, 0.9, 0.25, 0.75, 0.5

Page 29: 0.25 + 0.5 = 1/4 + 1/2 = 3/4
0.5 + 0.75 = 1/2 + 3/4 = 1 1/4
0.75 + 0.75 = 3/4 + 3/4 = 1 1/2
1.2, 2.0, 1.1, 3.5, 1.4, 0.5, 1.8, 1.0.